A M

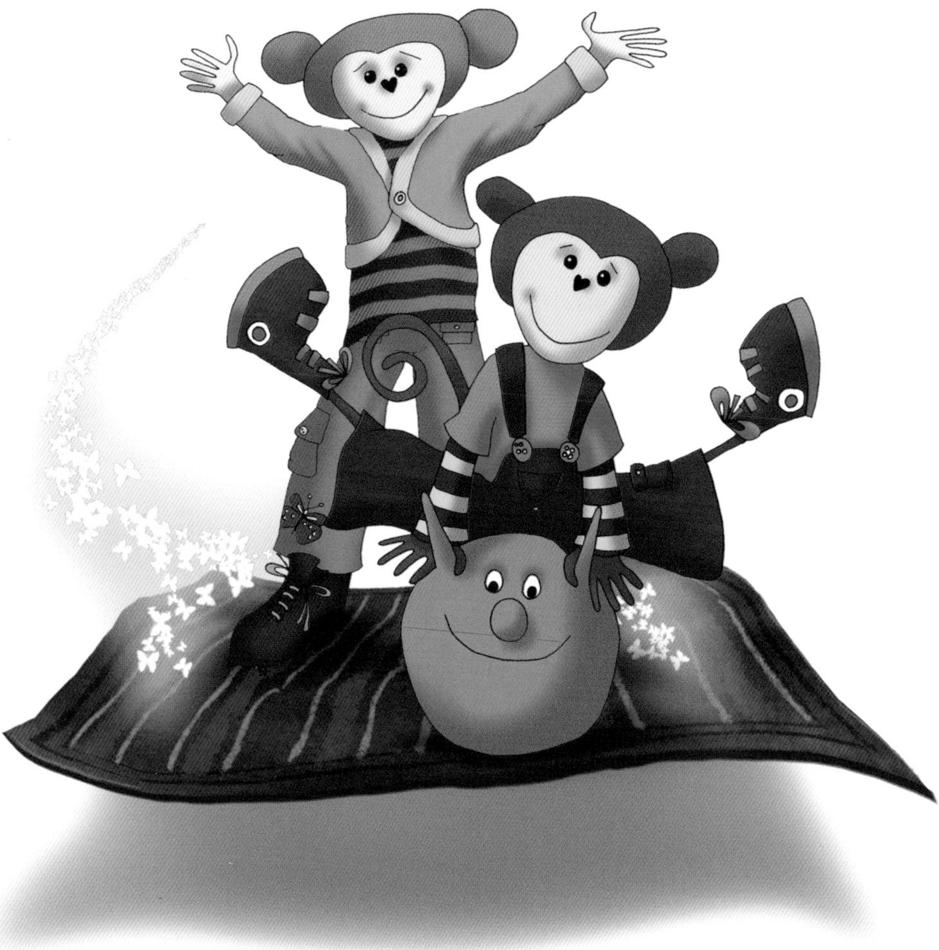

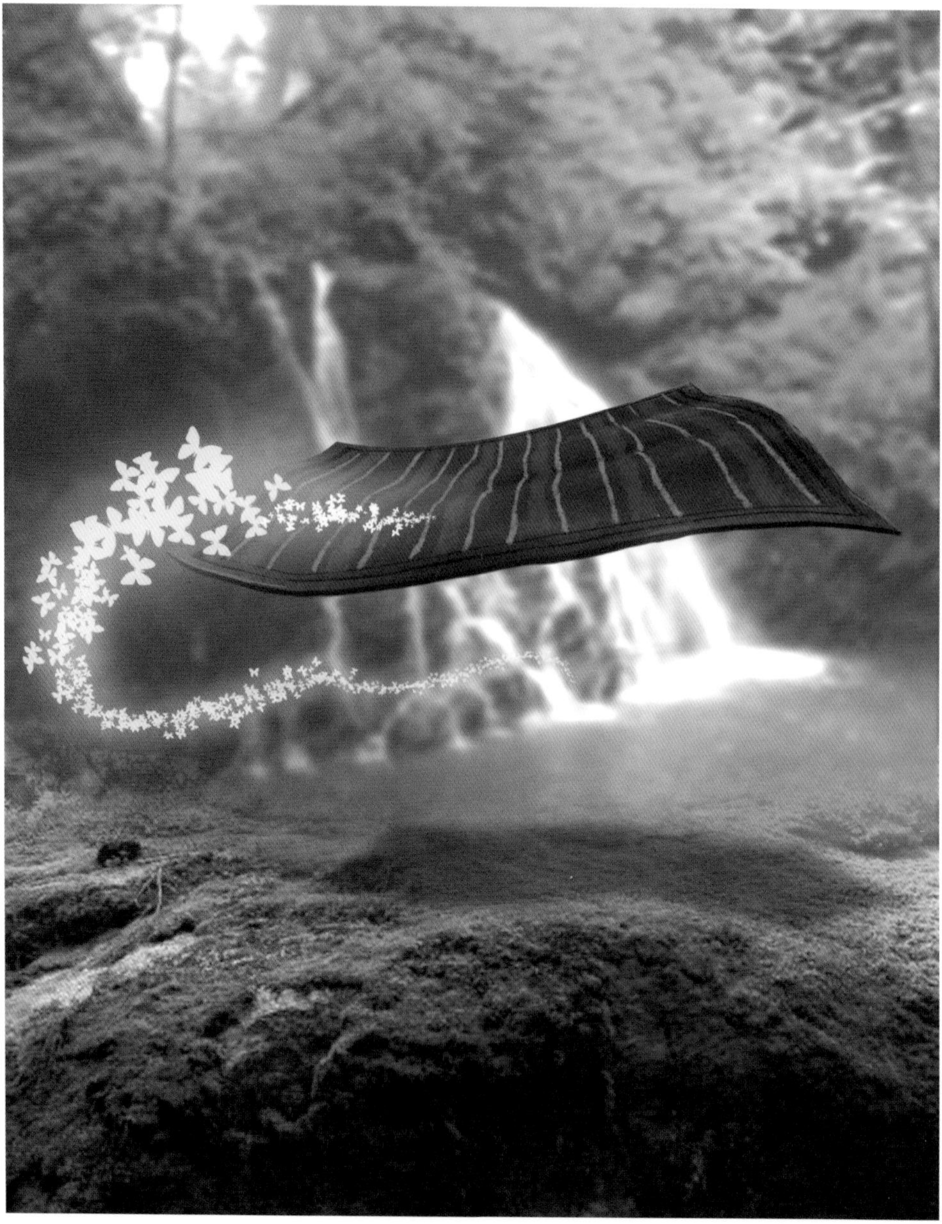

"I am a mat."

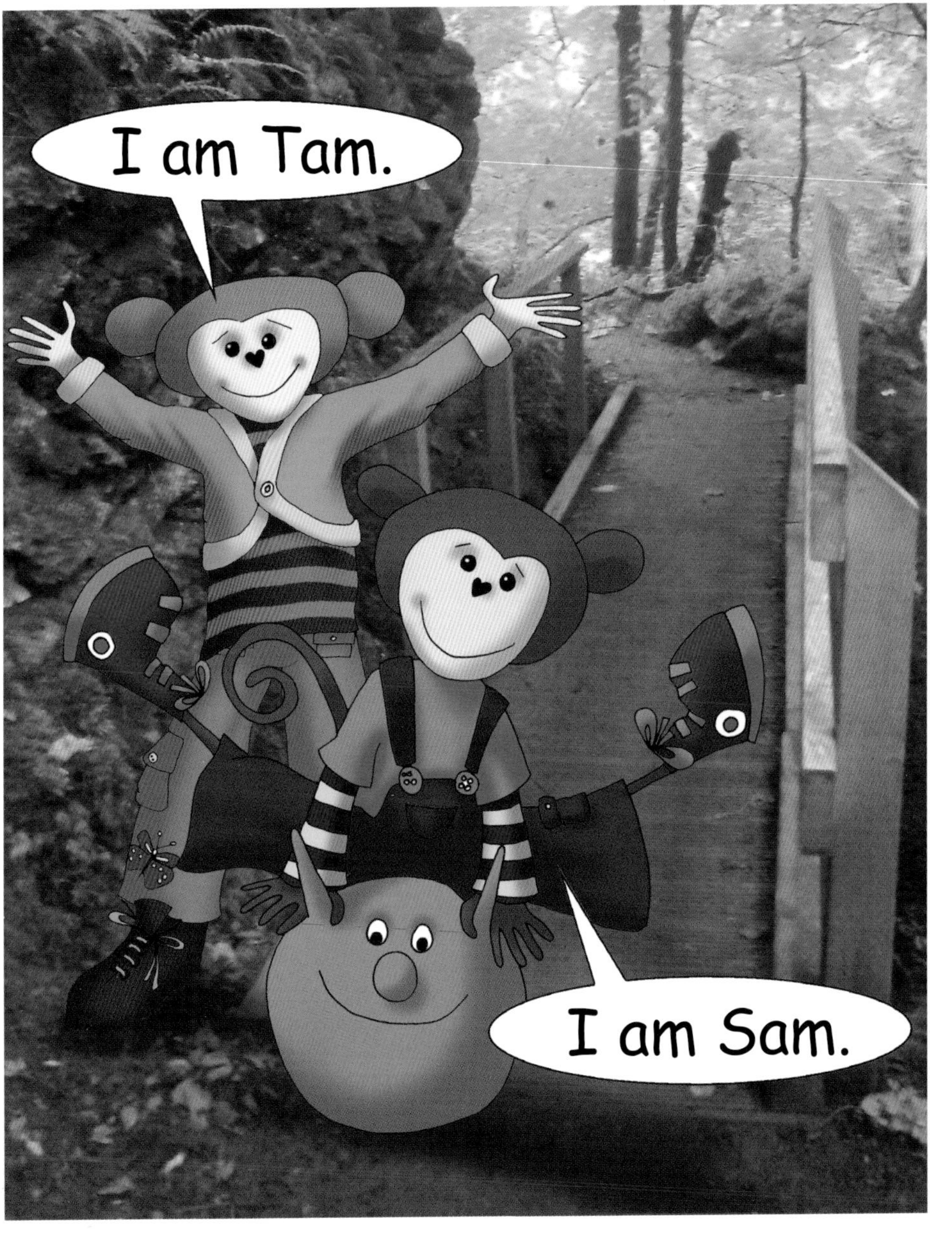

"I am Tam." "I am Sam."

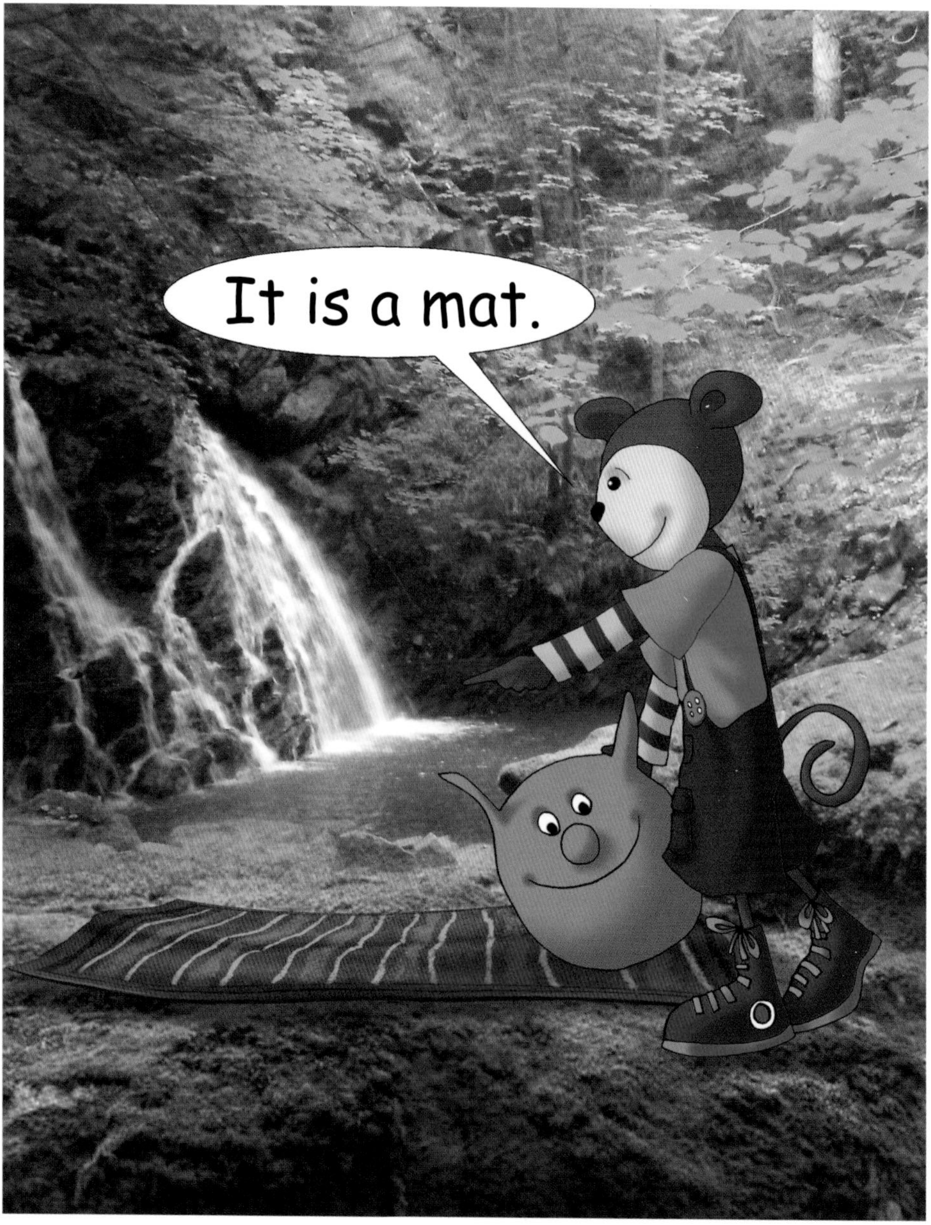

"It is a mat."

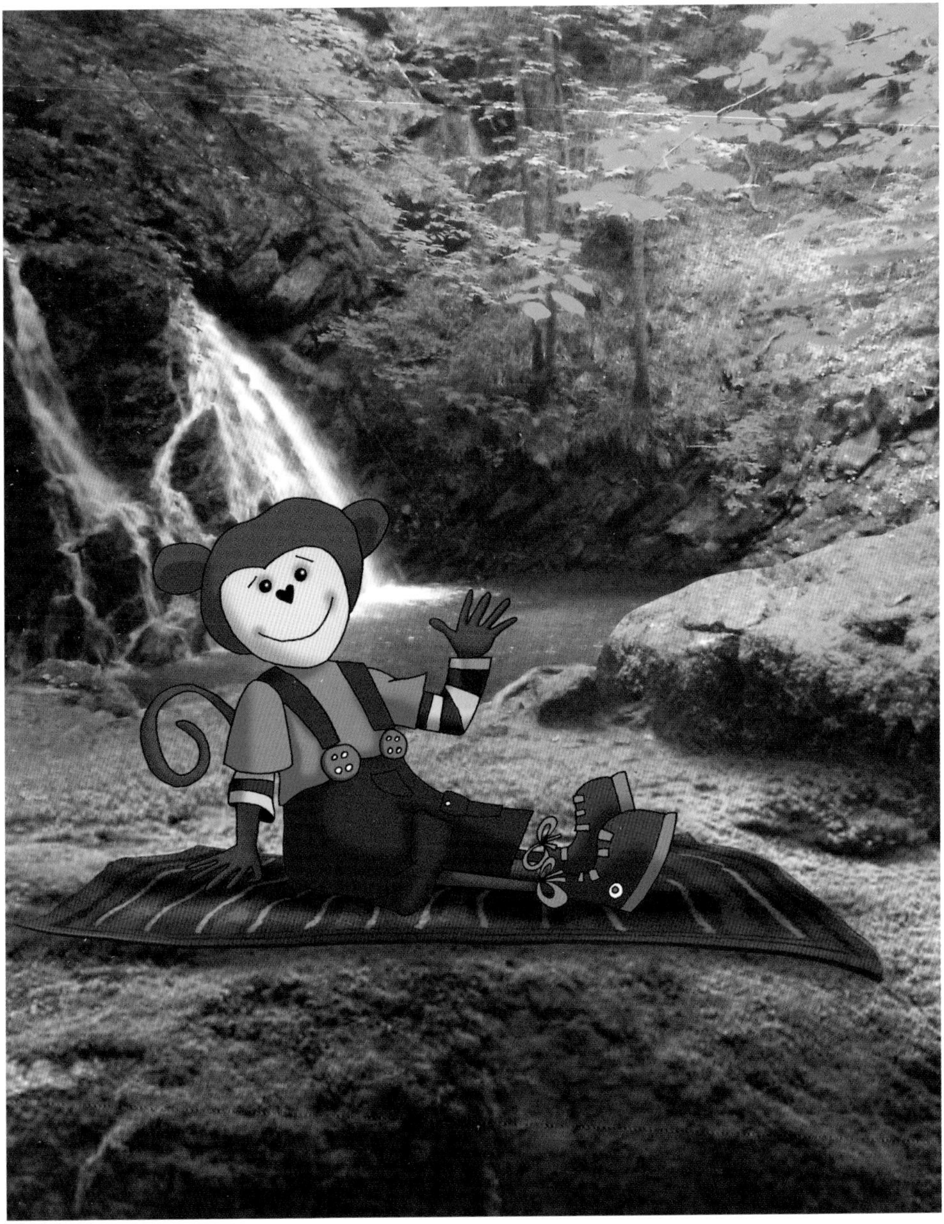

Sam sat.

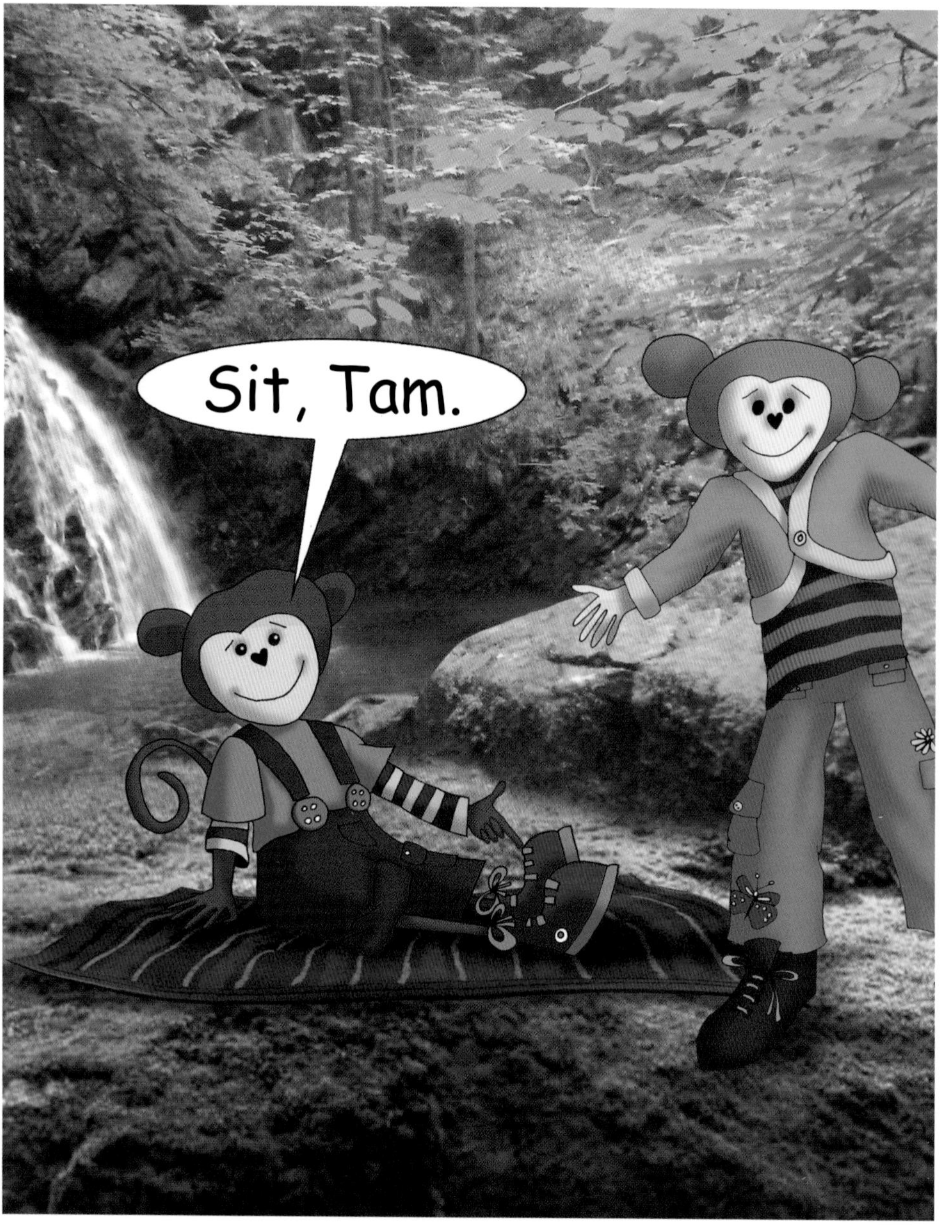

"Sit, Tam."

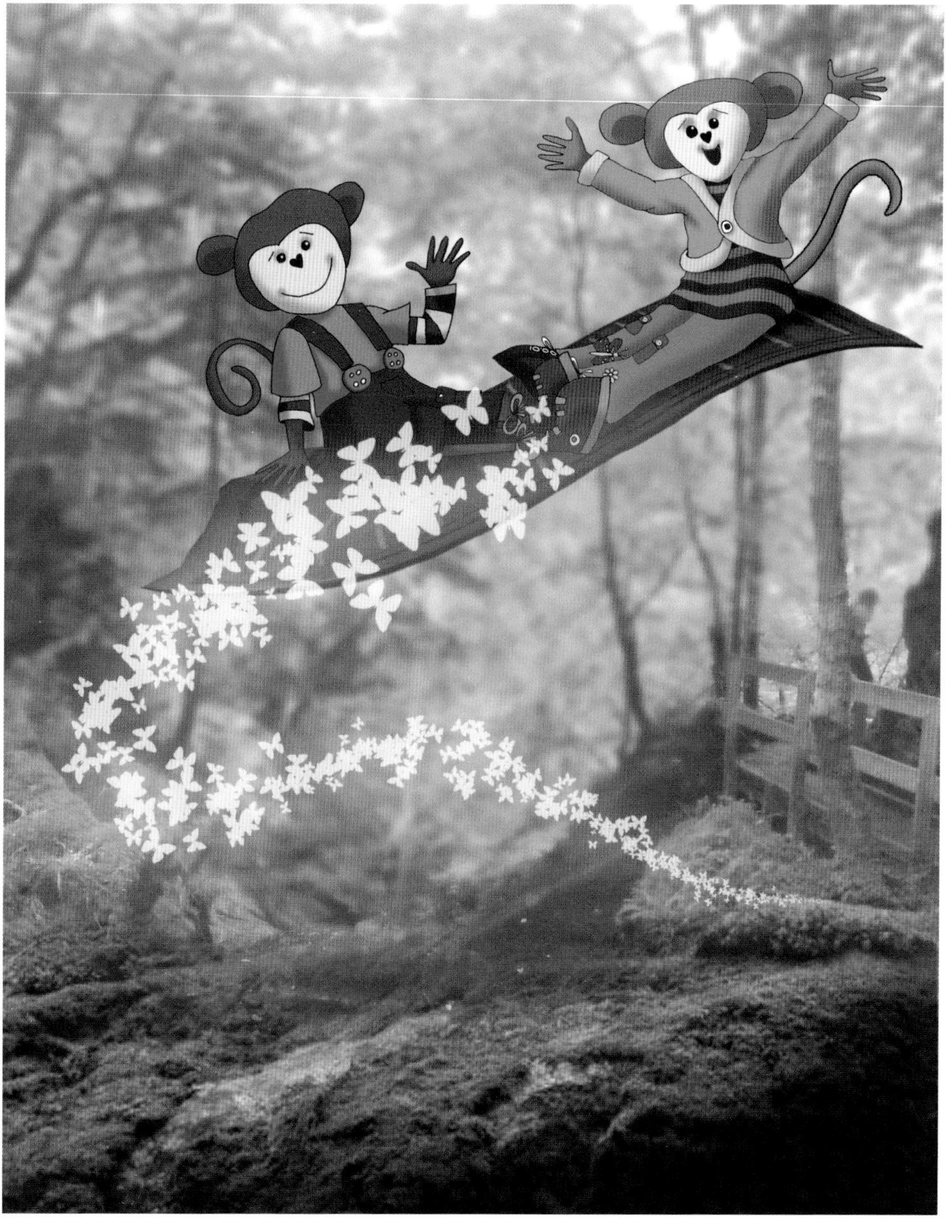

Tam sat.

Reading and Spelling Practice

at	mat
it	Tam
am	sit
Sam	sat

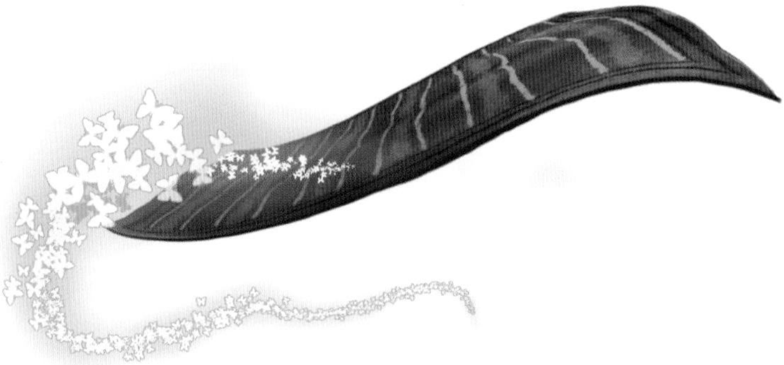